THE
Scottish
COOK

THE
Scottish
COOK

Written by
Judy Paterson

Illustrated by Fiona Lang

Birlinn

THE *Scottish* COOK

First published 1995

BIRLINN LIMITED
13 Roseneath Street
Edinburgh EH9 1JH

A CIP record for this book is available
from the British Library

ISBN: 1 874744 35 1

© Text and cover illustrations by
Fiona Lang

Text layout and cover design by
Smith & Paul Design Associates, Paisley

Printed & bound by ORIENTAL PRESS, (DUBAI).

Contents

Acknowledgements

To those who have offered advice and criticism, help and
encouragement, many thanks.

Dedication

To Mike, with love, as always
To Jos, with love. F.L.

Introduction

The 'Traditional Recipes' of Scotland date mostly from the eighteenth and nineteenth centuries, having been handed down through Household books, Memoirs and Journals. They reflect regional differences, the way of life, the availability of produce and commodities, and of course, the seasons.

The gradual opening up of the remote Highlands, the introduction of the turnip and the potato, had profound effects on the Scots diet. Oats became less important as the staple food and meat became available throughout the year.

The Highland Clearances, which banished crofters and clansmen to make way for sheep, saw farmers driven to the coast. Many took up fishing. Many of course, left Scotland for the New World.

> "The teeth of the sheep shall lay the plough on the shelf."
> Thomas the Rhymer

Traditions in curing fish are as old as the Norse Invasion and Scottish humour is encapsulated in the way a fat Loch Fyne herring is known as a Glasgow Magistrate!

Scotland's National poet, Robert Burns wrote the world famous *Address to the Haggis* and Sir Walter Scott made a heroine of one Mistress Margaret Dods of the Cleikum Inn, in his novel *St. Ronan's Well*.

Isobel Christian Johnston, the enterprising wife of an Edinburgh Publisher, parodied Scott's style and presented a collection of recipes under the pseudonym, Meg Dods. It is one of the most important and delightful sources of the traditions of Scottish cookery, well 'larded' with anecdotes and advice from various members of the gastronomic 'Cleikum Club'. Through them she speaks about food, and most significantly, the Cook!

> "They know their own value: they are a privileged class;
> they toil in a fiery environment;
> they live under heavy responsibility."

Soup

"This is the comfortable pot au feu of Scotland... the pot luck of homely and hearty old-world hospitality." **Meg Dods**

Like its counterpart in many rural areas throughout Europe, this thick soup was actually a meal in itself. It was frequently made in quantities large enough to last a couple of days. Sometimes the meat was removed and served separately. Cooked slowly in a large pot over the open hearth it was served at lunchtime, shared alike by the household and its servants. Recipes for this soup have been handed down for over two hundred years and each household probably varied it according to taste and means.

Scotch Broth

1lb (450g) neck or shoulder of lamb, fat trimmed
3 pints (1.7 litres) water
1oz (25g) pearl barley
2oz (50g) dried peas, soaked
1 large carrot and similar quantity of turnip, diced
1 large onion, diced
The white of a leek, sliced
4oz (100g) shredded white cabbage
Chopped parsley
Salt and pepper

Put the meat, barley, and soaked peas in the water in a large pan with seasoning and bring to the boil. Skim if necessary, cover and simmer for about an hour.

Add all the vegetables, except the cabbage, and simmer for a further 30 minutes. Add the cabbage and simmer for another 15 minutes.

Remove the meat and chop a suitable quantity, returning it to the pan for a hearty soup. Serve the soup hot with a garnish of parsley. Dumplings or Hodgils may be served with this to make a meal.

Variations

Substitute Beef : Brisket is ideal if you wish to reserve the meat for slicing afterwards, either hot or cold. Hough is flavoursome and will 'shred' well to make a thick stew-like soup, but it will require longer cooking.

Use chicken or game, or even a combination of meats. Grated carrot may be substituted for the cabbage if preferred.   Serves 6-8

Hodgils

4oz (100g) oatmeal
Salt and pepper
Chopped chives (optional)
Fat, skimmed from the broth for binding

Mix together thoroughly and shape into small balls. cook for 20 minutes in the simmering soup.

Hotch Potch

1½lb (675g) trimmed neck of lamb, and/or
A marrow bone
4 pints (2.2 litres) of water
Salt
3 young carrots, scraped and diced
3 sweet white turnips, pared and diced
6 spring onions, chopped
8oz (225g) fresh shelled peas
4oz (100g) prepared young broad beans
1 medium head of cauliflower, cut into florets
1 small lettuce, washed and chopped
Chopped parsley

Place the meat (and /or bones) into a large pan with salt and the water and bring to the boil, skimming the surface as required. Add the carrots, turnips, broad beans, onions and half of the peas and simmer for an hour.*

Add the cauliflower, lettuce and remaining peas and cook for a further 30 minutes.

Remove the meat (and bones) and serve hot, garnished with chopped parsley.

*Cooking Times: Some traditional recipes suggest cooking for three or four hours to maximise the flavours of the ingredients. They also suggest the soup should be of a thick consistency.   Serves 8-10

Cock-A Leekie

1 large boiling fowl
10 leeks, thoroughly cleaned and sliced
6 pints (3.5 litres) stock
Salt and pepper
Chopped parsley

Put the fowl and half of the leeks into a large pan and add the stock. Bring to the boil and then simmer gently for 2-3 hours, or until the fowl is tender.

Remove the fowl and draw off the grease. Add the rest of the leeks and simmer for another 15 minutes or so until the leeks are just tender. Adjust the seasoning and add some of the chopped fowl. Serve very hot with a garnish of parsley.

The quantities given are for a large party. It is the traditional soup to serve at a Burns supper, for instance. To serve 6-8, use $\frac{1}{2}$ a fowl or two chicken joints, and halve the other ingredients.

Popularly believed to be named after Mary of Lorraine, mother of Mary Stuart, Lorraine Soup is a nice celebration of Auld Alliance between Scotland and France.

"Sir, I am above National Prejudice and I must say I yield to the scots superiority in all soups - save turtle and oxtail and mulligatawny. An Antiquarian friend of mine attributes this to their early and long connection with the French — a nation pre-eminent in soups."

Touchwood - The Cleikum Club

14

Lorraine Soup

1lb (450g) cooked white meat of chicken
2oz (50g) blanched almonds
1 tablespoon fresh white breadcrumbs
Pared rind of $\frac{1}{2}$ a lemon
Salt and pepper
Chopped parsley
2 cooked egg yolks
3 pints (1.7 litres) chicken stock
Pinch of mace
$\frac{1}{4}$ pint (150ml) single cream

Into a liquidizer or blender put the chopped white meat,
the almonds and a little of the stock. Blend. Add the
breadcrumbs with more of the stock and the egg yolks.
Blend again. (Or traditionally you may like to use a
pestle and mortar!).

Put these ingredients into a saucepan and combine with
the rest of the stock. Add seasonings to taste and the
lemon rind. Bring to the boil slowly, stirring constantly.
Just before serving, remove the lemon rind and add the
cream. Reheat carefully without boiling.

Serve in warmed soup plates with a garnish of chopped
parsley. Serves 6-8

15

The *"Fisherrow Medallion"* was presented to the men of Fisherrow, the fishing village of Musselburgh, in 1796 to acknowledge their role in defending Scotland against the threat of French Invasion during the Napoleonic Wars.

16

This simple soup was available at street stalls and was often the treat which young lads would buy their sweethearts as they strolled in Musselburgh of a Sunday evening.

Mussel Brose

50 mussels, washed and scrubbed.
(Discard any that are open)
1 pint (600ml) water
1 pint (600ml) milk, or fish stock
Salt and pepper
1oz (25g) toasted oatmeal

Put the mussels into a pan with the water, cover and cook quickly over a high heat for a couple of minutes. Give the mussels a quick stir to allow the unopened ones to fall to the bottom of the pan. Cover and cook for a further couple of minutes. Do not over cook.

Strain the liquor and reserve. Shell and beard the mussels. Heat up the milk, (or the fish stock), and add the mussel liquor and bring to the boil. Add the mussels and keep the Brose hot but not cooking as this could toughen the mussels. Add a cupful of the brose to the oatmeal, stirring quickly so that it forms knots. Add the mix to the soup. Do not boil.   Serves 4-6

Game Soup

Adapted from Meg Dods 'Superlative Game Soup'

Any carcasses - hare, rabbit, venison or game birds.
4 rashers streaky bacon
1 onion stuck with three cloves
1 parsnip diced
1 tablespoon chopped parsley
A pinch or two of allspice
1-2oz (25-50g) butter
2 carrots diced
$\frac{1}{2}$ a head of celery sliced
Salt and freshly ground black pepper
4 pints (2.2 litres) of beef stock

Brown the bacon with any uncooked game. Put all the cooked meats into a large pan with the onion. Saute the vegetables in the butter and add to the pan. Add the seasonings, parsley and stock. Bring to the boil and simmer gently for $1\frac{1}{2}$ hours.

Remove the carcasses and bacon. Discard the cloves. Puree the soup with the vegetables in a blender. Return to a clean pan and add any pieces of meat stripped from the carcasses. Meg Dods suggests the bacon should be discarded.

Bring the soup to boiling point before serving.

Serves 8-10

Fish

Ham 'N' Haddie

Traditionally these two ingredients were fried together but ingenuity is also traditional in Scotland so there are a number of ways in which this north eastern dish might be prepared. 'Ham' in Scotland, by the way, generally refers to bacon, often termed gammon. 'Cooked ham' is the term used for what is usually called by the English, ham.

> 2 Finnan Haddock (or other lightly smoked haddock)
> 8oz (225g) smoked bacon (or unsmoked if preferred)
> Pepper and butter

Lightly poach the haddock in a small amount of water, skin down, for a couple of minutes. Turn and cook for a further couple of minutes. Remove the fish skin and the bones.

Cook the bacon in a frying-pan, turning once and then adding the fish on top. Sprinkle with freshly ground black pepper, cover and simmer for a few minutes.

Serves 2

"Haddies is men's lives"
The invariable plea of the Newhaven Fishwives.

Potted Herring

6 or 8 herring fillets
Salt and freshly ground black pepper
6-8 black peppercorns
2 cloves
1 bay leaf
Pinch of mace
Small onion very finely shredded
Sufficient water and vinegar in equal parts for cooking
Oven: 325F / 170C / Gas 3

Sprinkle the fillets with salt and pepper. Roll them up, skin side out from the tail end, and pack them in a shallow ovenproof dish. Sprinkle over the spices and the onions. Pour over just enough water and vinegar mixed, to cover the fish. Cover the dish.

Bake for 45 minutes and then remove the cover and cook for a further 15-20 minutes.

Serve cold with potato salad.

Serves 6-8

From the early 15th century the herring was regarded as a source of employment and wealth. David II was the first to impose an export duty on the migratory fish which later became immortalised by Neil Gunn as the "Silver Darlings"

"In a house down a stair in Broughton Street... one might obtain at a modest charge of sevenpence, a liberal helping from a succulent dish called salmon hash, better known as, Tweed Kettle."   James Bertram.

Tweed Kettle

2lb (1kg) fresh salmon
2 tablespoons shallots or chives, chopped
$\frac{1}{4}$ pint (257ml) dry White Wine
1oz (25g) butter
Pinch of mace
$\frac{1}{4}$ pint (150ml) water
4oz (100g) button mushrooms chopped
Salt and pepper
Chopped parsley

Simmer the salmon in the water with the salt, pepper and mace for about five minutes. Take the salmon out and reserve the stock. Remove the skin and bones and cut the salmon into chunky cubes. Return the fish to the stock with the wine and shallots, bring to simmering point gently and cook for 15-20 minutes.

Cook the chopped mushrooms in butter until soft and add to the salmon. Season further if required. Add the parsley and serve with hot mashed potatoes.

Serves 6

TROUT

"Brown had caught some excellent trout and cooked them with oatmeal..."

Queen Victoria
Leaves from a Journal of Our Life in the Highlands. (1846-61)

Lightly salt the trout and allow to stand for 12-24 hours. Before cooking wipe dry with kitchen paper, sprinkle with salt and pepper, dip in milk and roll in oatmeal.

Cook quickly in hot oil, turning once so that the sides are lightly browned.
Serve with a dot of butter and wedges of lemon.

"Butter and Burn trouts are kittle meat for maidens."

Old Scots saying.

Salmon

"This fish was so common an item of food, that stipulations were made by Scottish servants against having it above three times a week."

Meg Dods

Poached Whole Salmon

There are several ways in which this may be prepared. If you like salmon and entertain often, it may be advisable to invest in a fish kettle.

> A whole salmon, cleaned and wiped dry
> Court bouillon, or cube
> Garnish as chosen, see below

Lay the salmon gently into the pan (or on the strainer of a fish kettle) and pour in sufficient stock to cover. Bring to the boil and simmer gently for ten minutes per pound of fish.

Allow 4-6 oz per person

Alternatives

- Replace the stock with well salted cold water only.
- Use cold water, salted, to which you may add 2-3 tablespoons of Cider, or other light vinegar and a bouquet garni.

To Serve Hot

Drain carefully and lay the fish on a warm plate. You may like to remove the skin but Meg Dods regards this as 'bad practice'. Hot salmon may be served with melted butter, or hollandaise sauce. Garnish with twists or fans of lemon and springs of parsley. The carver should serve each person with a slice of the thicker part and also with a slice of the thin part.

To Serve Cold

Allow the fish to cool in the liquor. Drain thoroughly, skin the salmon and lay it on a plate. It may be garnished with wafer thin 'scales' of cucumber, or more simply with slices of lemon. Use parsley or mustard and cress and shredded lettuce to set the fish off. You may like to place half a stuffed olive in the eye socket. Serve with a home-made mayonnaise.

Salmon Steaks

To Grill: Set the grill-pan or other suitable dish under the grill to get hot. Dust the steaks with seasoned flour. Set butter to melt in the grill-pan and when bubbling add the salmon, coating each side well. Cook for about 8 minutes, basting if necessary. You should not have to turn the steaks. The flesh will be firm and pull away easily from the bone when it is done.

A little lemon juice sprinkled over the steaks as they cook, or added to the melted butter, improves flavour and adds moisture.
Serve with parsley butter.

Parsley Butter

Cream 4oz (100g) butter and add 2 tablespoons chopped parsley, 1 teaspoon lemon and freshly ground black pepper.

Roll into a thick tube. Chill and cut slices as required.

To Bake

Dip the steaks into seasoned flour and lay them in a well buttered dish. Add one of the following sauces, cover, and bake in a moderate oven for about half an hour.

Sauces for Salmon

Sauce Macleod

4 tablespoons double cream; 2 tablespoons dry sherry; 1 teaspoon anchovy essence; a very little cayenne pepper and salt and pepper to taste.

Mix the ingredients and cover the steaks. Serve with thick wedges of lemon and a light shake of paprika to colour the sauce.

Simple Sauce

$\frac{1}{2}$oz (15g) butter; $\frac{1}{2}$oz (15g) cornflour;
salt and pepper $\frac{1}{2}$ pint (300ml) milk, or milk and fish stock; lemon juice.

Melt the butter and work in the cornflour. Add the liquid and blend carefully. Over a low heat, stir and bring to the boil. Adjust the seasoning. Pour over the salmon and cook as above. Garnish with lots of colour.

Variations on the above sauce follow. Make up your own names and add ingredients to give a distinctive Scottish flavour.

Mustard

Add 2 teaspoons dry mustard mixed with 2 teaspoons white vinegar.

This recalls our strong links with Scandanavia. Call it Viking sauce.

Arran Sauce

Add a heaped tablespoon of prepared whole grain
mustard and a tablespoon of whisky.

Seafarer's

Add 2-3 teaspoons anchovy essence to the sauce.

Traditional

Add chopped hard boiled egg.

Fennel

Add up to 2 tablespoons of chopped fennel and a
good tablespoon of butter.
This was a traditional sauce.

White Wine

Substitute $\frac{1}{4}$ pint (150ml) dry White Wine and
$\frac{1}{4}$ pint (150ml) fish stock for the liquid.
Call it Sauce Alliance.

Smuggler's

To the white wine sauce add 2 tablespoons of
Brandy, a tablespoon of chopped parsley,
2 teaspoons of lemon juice and 2 tablespoons of
double cream.

Meats, Game & Fowl

Venison Steaks

Venison Steaks
Butter and olive oil

Warm a covered dish in the oven for the cooked steaks.
Venison is very lean and will dry out quickly if over-
cooked. The best method is to slightly undercook and to
finish off in the oven while preparing the sauce.

Heat a heavy based pan and the butter and oil to very
hot. Add the steaks sealing quickly on both sides. Reduce
the heat and cook to taste, remembering that venison is
usually served pink. (3-4 minutes per side for medium).
Remove the steaks to the warm dish, cover, and keep in
the oven to finish cooking.

Pan Sauce

Saute 6oz (175g) finely chopped shallots or onions in the
residue fats until they are soft. Add a glass of red wine
and cook on a high heat for a few minutes. Remove from
the heat and add a little salt and a liberal amount of
freshly ground black pepper. Add 2oz (50g) butter,
stirring it constantly.

Serve over the hot steaks, garnished with chopped
parsley.

This quantity serves 2.

Meg Dod's Venison Sauce

Sweet sauce: melt two tablespoons of redcurrant or rowan jelly in a $^{1}/_{4}$ pint (150ml) of good red wine.

Port Wine Sauce

$^{1}/_{2}$ pint (300ml) game stock
2oz (50g) butter
Glass of Port
Pan juices if available

Boil the Port to reduce it by half. Add the stock and bring back to simmering point. If you have pan juices from the steaks or a roast add them now. Add seasoning if required and more Port if liked. Bring back to simmering and then remove from the heat. Stir in the butter gradually and thoroughly.

Ruby Wine Sauce

$^{1}/_{2}$ pint (300ml)   Glass of Red wine
Game stock   2 tablespoons Brandy
1 tablespoon rowan jelly   Salt and pepper
Lemon juice

Boil stock and wine on a high heat for a few minutes to reduce the liquid to about $^{1}/_{4}$ pint (150ml). Lower the heat and add the rowan jelly, the Brandy and the lemon juice. Taste and season as desired.

Scots Roast Grouse

2 Grouse of the same sex
  and weight and their livers,
  if possible
2oz (50g) butter
Salt and pepper
Flour
Extra butter for basting

Watercress to garnish
Lemon juice
Streaky bacon
2 slices of toast
Cayenne, (optional)

Oven: 400F/200C/Gas 6

Wipe the birds, inside and out, with kitchen paper. Blend
the butter with the lemon juice and the salt and pepper.
Divide into two portions and place in the body of each
bird. Wrap them well with the fatty bacon and lay them
on their sides in a roasting tin. Make a domed cover of
foil which will allow the air to circulate but will help
prevent drying. Cook for 30-45 minutes depending on
the size of the birds.

After 10-15 minutes, turn the birds to the other side,
baste with more butter. 10 minutes before serving,
remove the bacon, baste, sprinkle the flour over the birds
and set them on their backs for the last few minutes
cooking without the foil cover.

While the grouse cooks, prepare the livers by simmering
gently in a little water for 10 minutes. Mash or blend
them with a little salt and pepper and a tiny amount of
cayenne if liked. Spread on to two slices of toast and set
the grouse on top. Garnish with watercress.   Serves 2

Traditionally grouse is served with deeply fried, wafer thin rounds of potatoes and clear gravy or Bread Sauce.

Bread Sauce

This is one of the few truly Scottish sauces. It is only good when given the maximum time to absorb the flavours of the spices. It may be served with any fowl or feathered game.

1 medium onion, stuck with 4 cloves	2 tablespoons thick cream
³/₄ pint (450ml) milk	4 peppercorns
4oz (100g) good quality white bread crumbs	1 bay leaf
1oz (25g) butter	Salt and white pepper
	Pinch of nutmeg

Place the onion in a pan with the milk, butter, peppercorns and bayleaf. Bring to just under boiling point and keep it hot for ¹/₂ an hour. Remove from the heat, cover and let it stand a further ¹/₂ hour to infuse. Strain the milk into a clean pan and stir in the breadcrumbs. Heat it gently to just under simmering, for 30 minutes, stirring frequently. Season to taste, and stir in the cream and nutmeg.

Jugged Hare

1 hare, jointed. Reserve the blood
6oz (175g) finely chopped bacon
3-4 small onions peeled, and each stuck with a clove
1 tablespoon lemon juice
2 bay leaves
Salt and freshly ground black pepper
$^{1}/_{4}$ pint (150ml) claret or port
Flour for thickening
2oz (50g) dripping or fat
1 stick celery chopped
3 carrots sliced
A bouquet garni
8 peppercorns
1$^{1}/_{2}$ pint (900ml) good stock
3 tablespoons redcurrant jelly
Oven: 350F/180C/Gas 4

Soak the joints in cold water with a little vinegar for
several hours. Wipe dry and brown them in the fat. Place
them in a large casserole, dusting the pieces with flour.
Add the bacon to the pan and fry lightly and then
transfer to the casserole with all the pan juices. Add all
the other ingredients. Cover tightly and cook for three
hours or until tender. Remove the bouquet garni and the
cloves from the onions.

If using the blood to thicken the gravy, spoon out a cupful
of gravy and allow it to cool. Mix in the blood and then

mix it through the casserole. Otherwise thicken with flour
and stock, in the usual manner. Stir in the redcurrant
jelly. Adjust the seasoning if required.

Garnish with stuffing balls and serve with extra
redcurrant jelly.   Serves 4-6

Stuffing balls

Combine 4oz (100g) fresh breadcrumbs with a medium
onion finely chopped, a bacon rasher finely chopped, a
pinch of mixed herbs, salt and pepper and a beaten egg.
Form small balls. Roll in egg and breadcrumbs and deep
fry until golden brown. Drain and keep warm and place
into the casserole as you are about to serve.

35

Haggis

The haggis is nothing more than the humble sausage of many a European country. A thrifty farmer's wife might sell the best cuts of lamb and use the rest to keep the family well fed. Robert Burns was responsible for it's popular survival into the 20th Century.

Haggis is traditionally made with the left-overs, the heart, liver and pluck (lungs) of the sheep. It requires the cleaning of the stomach bag into which the separately cooked, minced meats and other ingredients are stuffed. Prize-winning haggis is available from a number of outlets and it is rarely prepared in the average home nowadays.

"A haggis boiled for two hours may be kept for a week or two, and when cold, gets so firm that haggises are often sent from Scotland to distant places and countries"
Meg Dods

Try this recipe which is the real thing in terms of tradition and more than acceptable in terms of taste!

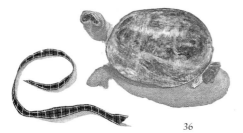

Haggis Royale

1½ lb (675g) leg of lamb coarsely minced
8oz (225g) shredded suet
2 egg yolks, beaten
¼ pint (150ml) Red wine
3 anchovy fillets, chopped
Zest from ½ a lemon
½ teaspoon cayenne
4oz (100g) minced onion (optional)
4oz (100g) pinhead oatmeal
4oz (100g) medium oatmeal
4oz (100g) crumbs of a granary loaf
2 tablespoons finely chopped parsley
2½ teaspoons white pepper
1½ teaspoons salt
Oven: 375F/190C/Gas 5

Combine all the ingredients thoroughly, pack into a bowl
(or two bowls) and cover the top tightly with foil. Bake for
1½ hours.   Serves 4-6

As Meg Dod's advises, "Serve hot as fire, with brown
gravy and venison sauce."

To Boil a Gigot with a Turnip

An adaptation from Meg Dod's Collection of Scottish National Dishes.

Legs of lamb generally weigh 4-5lb and will serve a party of eight, possibly with leftovers. The use of herbs was a matter of personal taste and those below may be altered or omitted. Nowadays, although not traditional, people also like to include onions. The amount of vegetables you use will depend upon the size of your pot. This recipe is served with caper sauce and dressed with carrots.

> 1 leg of lamb
> 2-3 onions, sliced (optional)
> Rosemary, thyme, parsley (optional)
> Salt
> 2-3 carrots, sliced thickly
> 1 turnip, peeled and cut in chunks
> 6-8 black peppercorns

Trim excess fat from the lamb and put it, and the other ingredients into a large saucepan and pour in enough cold water to reach about three-quarters of the pan. Cover and bring to the boil, at which point you should remove any scum. Simmer very gently for about 30 minutes per pound or until the meat is tender.

Remove the meat and keep hot. Strain the stock and separate the carrots and turnips. Skim the fat from the stock and reserve about $1\frac{1}{2}$ pints of stock for the sauce

Serves 8

Caper Sauce

2oz (50g) butter
1½ pints (900ml) lamb stock
Salt and pepper
2oz (50g) flour
3 tablespoons capers

Make a roux by melting the butter in a pan and
gradually stirring in the flour. Cook for almost a minute
on a low heat and then remove from the heat. Gradually
add about a cup full of stock stirring with a whisk all the
while to prevent forming lumps. Add the rest of the stock,
blend thoroughly and return to the heat adding capers.
Stir continuously as it heats through and thickens
slightly.

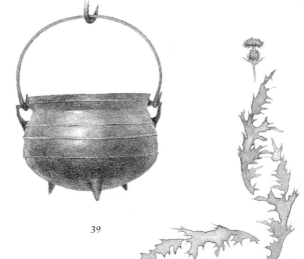

Stoved Howtowdie With Drappit Eggs

A chicken about 3lb (1.3kg)
4oz (100g) butter
6 peppercorns
Pinch allspice
Salt and pepper
1$\frac{1}{2}$-2lb (1kg) washed spinach
Chicken liver
6-8 pickling onions or 3 shallots
2 cloves
$\frac{1}{2}$ pint (300ml) chicken stock
1 egg per person
2 tablespoons double cream
Oven: 350F/180C/Gas 4

Stuffing

3oz (75g) fresh breadcrumbs
Pinch mixed herbs
2oz (50g) melted butter
1 small onion, chopped
1 tablespoon chopped parsely
Salt and pepper

Wipe the chicken, inside and out. Combine the ingredients for the stuffing and place inside the bird and truss it. Brown the chicken in the butter and place into a suitable casserole. Brown the onions and then add the spices and

40

stock. Bring to the boil and pour over the chicken. Cover and cook, for $1\frac{1}{2}$ hours or until the chicken is tender.

Cook and drain the spinach and keep hot.

Remove the chicken to a large serving dish and keep hot. Strain the stock and in a small amount of it poach the liver. Blend or sieve, and reserve.

Poach the eggs in the remaining stock, which must be then saved for the gravy. Arrange the eggs in nests of spinach around the chicken. Now combine the pureed liver with the rest of the stock to make a thick gravy. Pour some over the chicken and serve the rest separately.

Serves 4-6

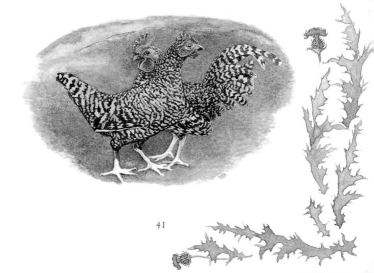

Eggs formed part of the rent, paid in kind to the Laird. Known as Kain Eggs they had to be of a certain size. This explains why eggs were not a common feature of Scottish cooking until the eighteenth century.

The recipe below uses Egg Sauce, an original Scottish variation on Bechemal sauce, and now a standard in British cooking.

Scots Chicken Fillets

2 breasts of chicken
Chicken stock

Egg Sauce
$\frac{1}{2}$ pint (300ml) milk
1oz (25g) butter
1oz (25g) plain flour
2 large hard-boiled eggs

Poach the fillets of the chicken in the stock for about 30 minutes or until cooked. Keep hot.

Make the sauce by melting the butter and stirring in the flour. Make up the milk to 3/4 pint (450ml) by adding some of the chicken stock. Gradually add to the butter and flour and over a low heat, stirring constantly, cook until the sauce is thickened.

Chop the whites of the eggs quite finely and add to the sauce. Pour sauce over the fillets and grate the egg yolks over the top.

42

Mince-Fowl

12-16oz (350g-450g) finely chopped cooked,
   white meat of chicken
1 pint (600ml) chicken stock
4 spring onions, chopped
Salt and pepper
3 tablespoons cream
4-6oz (100-175g) button mushrooms
4oz (100g) butter
2oz (50g) flour
Pinch of mace
Lemon juice
Chopped parsley

Wipe and slice the mushrooms and simmer gently, with
the spring onions, in 2oz (50g) butter in a covered pan
for about 10 minutes.

Melt the rest of the butter over a low heat and blend in
the flour, stirring constantly for a few minutes. Remove
from the heat and stir in some of the stock to make a
smooth paste. Blend in the rest of the stock and cook,
stirring all the while until thickened. Add the chicken and
the mushrooms with their juices, the mace and the
parsley. Check the seasoning and heat through gently.
Before serving add a good squeeze of lemon juice and the
cream. Stir thoroughly. Serve with rice or creamed
potatoes.   Serves 2-3

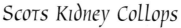

Scots Kidney Collops

2-3 Kidneys per person
Flour
2 teaspoons wine vinegar
Chopped parsley
1 tablespoon mushroom ketchup
1 small onion, minced
3oz (75g) butter
Salt and pepper
$^3/_4$ pint (450ml) hot water

Slice the kidneys into 'collops' or steaks and soak them in water for ten minutes. Dry them, dust with flour and brown in melted butter.

Add the minced onion, salt, pepper and some chopped parsley and pour over the hot water. Add the vinegar.

Cover the pan and simmer very gently for 1/2 an hour or so until the kidneys are cooked.

Add mushroom ketchup and thicken the gravy with a little paste of flour and water, mixed.

Serve garnished with chopped parsley.

Serves 2

Scotch Minced Collops

1lb (450g) minced steaks
$\frac{1}{2}$ pint (300ml) beef stock
1 medium onion, minced
1 tablespoon mushroom ketchup
1 tablespoon butter
1 tablespoon oatmeal
Salt and pepper

Gently sweat the onions in the butter until soft and add the minced meat stirring continuously to ensure there are no lumps.

Add the seasonings and stir in the oatmeal. Finally add the stock. Simmer gently for about $\frac{1}{2}$ an hour.

Serve on toast or with mashed potatoes.

Serves 2-3 generously

This is a simple and homely dish. It may be made with minced venison or minced hare. Adjust the seasonings to suit the choice of meat.

Venison Pasty

2lb (900g) trimmed and diced shoulder venison
$\frac{1}{4}$ pint (150ml) red wine vinegar
$\frac{1}{2}$ pint (300ml) good stock
Salt and pepper
Pinch of allspice
$\frac{1}{4}$ pint (150ml) Red Wine or Port
2 onions finely sliced (optional)
Pinch of mace
$\frac{1}{2}$lb (225g), or more puff pastry
Oven: 450F/ 230C/ Gas8

Place the meat into a saucepan with the spices, wine and vinegar and the onions if used. Stir thoroughly and add sufficient stock to cover the meat. Simmer gently for $1\frac{1}{2}$ hours or until the meat is tender. Using a slotted spoon remove the meat and place into a deep pie dish. Thicken the gravy and add a suitable amount to the meat, up to $\frac{1}{2}$ inch (10mm) from the top of the dish.

Cover with puff pastry and make three of four slits in the top. Brush with milk and bake for 25-35 minutes.

Serves 6-8

Vegetables

Kale (borecole), a leafy winter green, formed the staple of the old Scots diet. Many sayings attest to its importance in daily life: so when a man was fortunate his neighbours might say,

"He's got his head in a gude kale pot!"

Cabbage replaced kale and the potato became a staple in most homes. Broccoli, endives, celery, cauliflower, along with the less hardy tomato and lettuce were only cultivated in the gardens of the wealthy, but by the nineteenth century vegetables such as cabbage, carrots, peas, beans, onions and leeks were available quite widely.

The turnip was originally used as a dessert by the wealthy. Its cultivation as fodder for livestock ensured a supply of meat all year. The humble "neep" also went into the cooking pot and today remains a feature of traditional cookery.

Vegetables

"Some humorous writer pited those people who lived before the publication of the Waverly Novels and the introduction of potatoes."

Meg Dods

Stoved Potatoes

8-10 medium potatoes (mealy ones are best)
3 medium onions, thinly sliced
2 tablespoons beef dripping, or butter
Salt and pepper
$\frac{1}{2}$ pint (300ml) water

Peel the potatoes and slice evenly and thickly. Melt the dripping or butter in a heavy saucepan and fry the onions until lightly coloured and soft. Add the potatoes, seasoning well. Add the water, bring to simmering point and cover tightly, cooking over a low heat for about an hour.

Shake the pot occasionally to prevent sticking. Check after the hour. You should not have to add any more water. Cook for a further $\frac{1}{2}$ hour. Serve on its own as a supper dish or as an accompaniment to meat dishes.

Lang Kail

Curly kail, butter, salt and pepper, water

Strip the leaves from the stems and remove any tough fibres. Wash well and boil rapidly in plenty of well salted water for 20-30 minutes. Drain well and puree. Heat with butter and season with salt and pepper. Serve very hot with beef or pork or other meats.

Clapshot– An Orkney Dish

1lb (450g) potatoes, peeled and diced
Chives (optional)
Salt and pepper
3/4 lb (350g) turnips, peeled and diced
1oz (25g) butter or dripping

Boil the turnip for 15 minutes and then add the potatoes
and boil until cooked. Drain well. Add the chives, butter
and seasonings. Mash thoroughly and serve very hot.
Always have a larger amount of potato than turnip or it
will be too sloppy.

Neeps or Neep Purry

Turnip
Butter
Salt and pepper
A pinch of ground ginger, (optional)

Take a suitable amount of turnip, peel and dice. Bring to
the boil in salted water and simmer, covered, for 15-20
minutes or longer. The turnip should be soft.

Drain well. Mash with butter, salt, pepper and ginger
and either keep hot in the oven or return to the pan to
make piping hot.

The almost bland Neeps are the traditional vegetable to
accompany spicy Haggis.

The introduction of the potato and cabbage gave rise to a simple recipe which varies regionally in minor ways. The names attached to such a homely dish attest to the imaginations of the Scottish cooks of bygone days.

Kailkenny - Aberdeenshire

Mash together equal quantities of boiled cabbage and boiled potatoes, season with salt and pepper and stir in a suitable quantity of cream, sufficient to make a smooth consistency. Serve very hot.

Rumbledethumps - Border District

Mash together equal quantities of boiled cabbage and boiled potatoes with butter salt and pepper. This may be put into a dish, covered with grated cheese and browned. Chopped cooked onions may be added.

Colcannon - Highlands

Use equal quantities of boiled cabbage and boiled potatoes; 2-3 boiled carrots; a medium turnip boiled. Chop the cabbage finely and mash all the other vegetables with butter. (Traditionally, dripping might be used.) Add the cabbage to the mashed vegetables and return to a pan with some melted butter, salt and pepper and stir until very hot. Serve as an accompaniment to meat, or, if serving as a supper dish, add a spoonful of good brown gravy.

Desserts

Traditions in sweet foods range from the elaborate to the simple seasonal treats of the countryside. Sugar and spices were expensive items and the skills required to make pastries and confections allowed a small industry to develop in places such as Edinburgh, where, on the High Street, in the 18th Century, women such as Mrs Fraser set up a school and also sold her famous creations.

In Rural areas harvest time brought a surfeit of fruits and rich cream and of all the traditional 'desserts' or sweets, Cranachan is probably the most famous. It exemplifies Scottish simplicity and the use of natural produce.

Cranachan

3-4oz (75-100g) slightly toasted and sifted oatmeal
10fl oz (300ml) double or whipping cream
1 tablespoon malt whisky
6oz (175g) raspberries or blackberries

Whip the cream. Pour the whisky over the oatmeal and fold the mixture into the cream. Fold in the fruit reserving a few pieces for decoration.
Serve in glasses, chilled.   Serves 4

At Hallowe'en small charms were stirred into the Cranachan brining the finders good luck.

Caledonian Cream

10fl oz (300g) double, or whipping cream
2 tablespoons brandy or malt whisky
2 tablespoons orange marmalade
1 tablespoon lemon juice
1oz (25g) castor sugar

Combine the brandy, marmalade, lemon juices and
sugar and add the cream last. Whip the mixture until it
is thick.

Spoon into glasses and chill before serving.   Serves 4

Iced Stapag

1 pint (600ml) double cream
Several drops vanilla essence
2 tablespoons castor sugar
2 heaped tablespoons coarse oatmeal

Whip the cream and add the flavouring and the sugar.
Set to freeze until the edges are beginning to ice. Stir well
and leave to almost freeze. Toast the oatmeal so that it is
dry but not browned.Stir it into the almost frozen cream
and return it again to the freezer.

To serve: remove from the freezer about $\frac{1}{2}$ an hour
before serving.   Serves 8-10

Traditional Cloutie Dumpling

3oz (75g) flour
3oz (75g) breadcrumbs
3oz (75g) chopped suet
1 teaspoon ground cinnamon
$^1/_2$ teaspoon ground ginger
2oz (50g) sultanas
2oz (50g) currants

2oz (50g) brown sugar
1 tablespoon syrup
$^1/_2$ teaspoon bicarbonate
of soda
About 6oz (170ml) freshly
soured milk or buttermilk

Mix all the ingredients to make a fairly soft batter. Dip a large piece of cotton cloth into boiling water; wring it and dredge with flour. Set the cloth into a basin and spoon in the batter. Draw up the cloth evenly, leaving a space to allow the pudding to swell, and tie tightly with string.

Put a plate into the bottom of the steaming pan and put the dumpling onto this. Pour boiling water up to $^3/_4$ the way up the dumpling and simmer for 2-2$^1/_2$ hours, adding more boiling water as required.

To serve the dumpling: remove from boiling water and dip into cold water for a second to prevent the dumpling sticking to the cloth. Put the dumpling into a bowl and remove the string and open out the cloth.Put a warmed plate over the top and invert. Remove the cloth carefully and if necessary, dry off in the oven. Dredge with caster sugar and serve with hot custard.

Apple Flory - Florentine Tart

8oz (225g) or more, puff pastry
2-3 apples, Bramleys for preference
1-2 tablespoons lemon juice
Orange or quince marmalade
1-2 teaspoons cornflour
3oz (75g) sugar
Grated rind of half a lemon
Cinnamon
Oven: 450F/230C/Gas 8

Line a tart dish with half the pastry and place in the refrigerator along with the rest of the pastry rolled to fit the top.

Peel, core, and thickly slice the apples, sprinkling with lemon juice as you go to prevent discolouration. Place the apples in a large saucepan with the sugar, a good pinch of cinnamon and the lemon rind and not quite enough water to cover them. Simmer gently until the apples begin to feel soft but are not mushy. Strain off the syrup and allow to cool.

Arrange the apples in the lined tart dish. Make a paste with the cornflour and a little of the cooled syrup. In a saucepan heat up a suitable amount of the syrup and add the cornflour paste, stirring to make a thick sauce. Spoon this over the apples. Spread a layer of marmalade over this and top with the remaining pastry. Seal the edges, make two or three slits in the top, brush with a little milk and bake in a quick oven at 450F/230C/Gas 8 for 15 minutes. Lower the heat to 400F/200C/Gas 7 and bake for a further 15 minutes.

Serve either hot or cold with whipped cream.   Serves 4-6

Scottish Flan

8oz (225g) puff pastry
Apricot jam
Preserved fruits of choice

With butter or margarine, grease a loose-bottomed fluted
flan dish and line it with puff pastry. (You could "Vandyke"
the edges by cutting points which should be shaped into rose
leaves). Bake blind.

Fill with any sort, or even a variety, of preserved fruits,
cherries, apples, apricots, pears. Melt a little apricot jam and
brush over the top to glaze.

Serves 4-6

To make a creamed flan

Make a rich custard and add any of the following ingredients
to suit the fruits you have chosen:

2oz (50g) ground almonds
Crushed ratafias
Orange or vanilla flavourings
Finely grated lemon rind
Rum or Brandy

Spread a thick layer of the cold custard in the cooked pastry
and arrange the fruit on the top. Glaze with a little melted
apricot jam

Serves 4-6

Scots Whipt Sillabubs

Adapted from Mrs Cleland's Recipe

    10fl oz (300ml) double or whipping cream
    Juice and finely grated rind of a lemon
    2 tablespoons caster suger (more or less, to taste)
    5fl oz (150ml) sweet sherry or dessert wine

Whip all the ingredients until stiff. Place in tall wine
glasses and chill for 12 hours before serving.

Serves 4-6

Edinburgh Fog

    10 fl oz (300ml) double or whipping cream
    1oz (25g) ratafia biscuits
    1oz (25g) blanched chopped almonds
    1oz (25g) caster sugar
    A few drops of vanilla essence

Whip the cream stiff with the sugar and vanilla essence.
Fold in the ratafias and almonds. Spoon into glasses and
decorate with extra almonds.

Serves 4

Victorian Steamed Pudding

These were many and varied and are still favourites today. The following basic recipe is called an Urney Pudding if you use strawberry jam, or Glister Pudding if you use marmalade.

    4oz (125g) self raising flour, sifted
    2 eggs, beaten
    4oz (125g) butter or margarine
    4oz (125g) sugar
    1 tablespoon of milk
    2 tablespoons of either strawberry jam or marmalade

Cream the butter and sugar and mix in the eggs. Gradually add the flour. Mix in the milk and the jam or marmalade. Put the mixture into a buttered basin leaving an inch or two at the top.

Cover with foil and tie with string. Place the bowl on a plate in a large pan. Fill with boiling water to $3/4$ the way up the bowl. Simmer for $1\frac{1}{2}$-2 hours, topping up with extra boiling water if required.   Serves 6

Scots Trifle

6 trifle sponges, split and spread with raspberry jam
4oz (100g) crumbed ratafia biscuits
Grated rind of $\frac{1}{2}$ a lemon
3fl oz (90ml) sweet sherry
2fl oz (60ml) brandy
20fl oz (600ml) thick custard
5fl oz (150ml) double or whipping cream
1 teaspoon caster sugar
Vanilla essence
Cherries, angelica and nuts to decorate

Place the sponges in the bottom of a glass trifle dish,
spread over the ratafias and lemon rind. Combine the
sherry and brandy and pour over. Leave to soak for a
while.

Beat the cold custard to a creamy consistency and spread
over the sponges.

Whip the cream with the vanilla essence and sugar and
spread over the custard. Decorate and serve chilled.

Serves 6-8

Bibliography

The Cook and Housewife's Manual : Mistress Margaret Dods
  R. Grant & Son, Bookseller. Edinburgh. 1854 (First published
  in 1826)

A New and Easy Method of Cookery: Elizabeth Cleland
  Edinburgh 1770

The Practice of Cookery, Pastry and Confectionery: Mrs Frazer
  Edinburgh 1820. First published 1771. "Sold at her house,
  Mil Sq., opposite the Tron Church

The Practice of Cookery adapted to the Business of Everyday
  Life: Mrs Dalgairns. Edinburgh 1829

The Cookery Book of Lady Clark of Tillypronie: ed. C. F. Frere
  Heinemann, 1909

The Scots Kitchen: F. Marion McNeill Blackie & Son 1929

Traditional Scottish Cookery: Theodora Fitzgibbon
  Fontana 1980

Scottish Regional Recipes : Catherine Brown
  Penguin 1983 - first published 1981

Broths to Bannocks Catherine Brown John Murray 1990

Memoirs of a Highland Lady: Elizabeth Grant of Rothiemurchas
  John Murray 1967

Memoirs of Lady Grisell Baillie: Countess of Ashburnham
  R & R Clark Edinburgh 1983 (4th ed)

Traditions of Edinburgh :Robert Chambers
  W & R Chambers 1869

The Good Scots Diet :Maisie Steven
  Aberdeen University Press. 1985

St Ronan's Well : Sir Walter Scott
  The Edinburgh Edition, William Paterson, 1887

Note for American Users

The American Pint is 16 fluid oz., while the British Pint is 20 fluid oz.

The American Tablespoon holds 14.2 ml compared to the British 17.7 ml.

The teaspoon measure is the same in both countries.

A general guide

8oz flour = 2 $\frac{1}{2}$ cups. Plain flour is known as All -purpose flour and Self- Raising Flour is known as All purpose self - raising flour.

8oz oatmeal, fine or medium = 2 cup

8oz Pinhead oatmeal = 2$\frac{1}{2}$ cups and is known as Irish oatmeal.

8oz sugar, granulated, caster = 1$\frac{1}{4}$ cups

8oz butter = 1 cup

8oz suet = 2 cups.

20fl oz = 2$\frac{1}{2}$ cups